HAPPY TO BE AN ASPIE

Welcome to my world

Printed in the United States of America

ISBN 978-1-7322570-0-9

First Printing 2018

Julia Dunbar
www.Happytobeanaspie.com
Happytobeanaspie@gmail.com

First Edition

Illustrations by Harvey Lanot
Harvey@lanotdesign.com

HAPPY TO BE AN ASPIE

Dedicated to Jillian, my wonderful
and courageous daughter.

Jillian and I dedicate this book
to Edward Dunbar, my father and
her grandfather, and my sister Dee Dee.
They would be so proud.
Thank you for always believing in and
supporting us. We miss you both.

Acknowledgements/Special Thanks:

I want to thank Harvey Lanot for his creativity and excellent illustrations and Jack Adler for his editing of my manuscript. It is important for me to list all the people who were involved in Jillian's education.

Special thanks to all the staff at Commerce Elementary. You witnessed Jillian's struggles and achievements. She was with you from kindergarten, and I appreciate your patience and all the tutoring you gave her after school during prime time. We love you all dearly.

A very, very special thanks to Mr. Graham (retired principal), who took the time to tutor Jillian during the summer after kindergarten because I couldn't afford the summer program.

I thank all Jillian's teachers: Mrs. Black, Mrs. Bison, Mr. Love, Mrs. Domico, and Mrs. Shanahan.

Mr. Bison, I will never forget the love, kindness, and support you showed over the years.

I am also grateful to the prime time teachers: Mrs. Rabaut, Mrs. Sken, Mrs. Nedwick, Mrs. Donna, Mrs. Krok, Mrs. Kelie, and Mrs. Sara.

I thank the principal, Mrs. Carlin, and special thanks go to Mrs. Denise Kaczmarek and Mrs. Kathy Williams.

Last but not least, thank you to Mrs. Traci Harp and Mrs. Julie Holloway for all the extra services you provided and for your love and kindness. Jillian will never forget you.

I continue to thank GOD for blessing me with two wonderful daughters and loving parents. Tay, I thank you for being the best big brother, thank you for always being there for the girls. I thank my family and friends for their support and encouragement.

Acknowledgements

To my best friend/niece, Micky, thank you for always supporting and believing in me. We have a special bond like no other, and I'm so grateful and blessed to have you. You are the first person I have ever shared my manuscripts and plays with. I love you.

To my niece Nikki, thank you for your love and support. Thank you for always being there for the girls and me. I love you.

Fay, I cannot thank you enough for helping me through all the rough times. Thank you for listening all those times when I cried on the phone out of frustration. Thank you for all the resources you shared with me. I could go on and on. I thank you, and I love you dearly.

TABLE OF CONTENTS

Julia Dunbar,
always a loving mother

TAY,
Jillian's protective brother

Lindsi,
Jillian's younger sister,
who she nicknamed Honie

CHAPTER I

"Mom"

When my daughter, Jillian, was eight years old, she was diagnosed with Asperger's/autism spectrum disorder (ASD). It was a devastating discovery, as it would have been for any parent, but it was especially shattering for me as a single mom. I comforted Jillian as best I could, although she didn't understand the fuss, and I vowed to make her world as happy, safe, and secure as possible. I've been with her every step of the way since the full realization that she was different and would face struggles throughout her life as a result of her condition.

I'll never forget the day she came home from elementary school and said, "Mommy, why don't people understand me?" We sat and cried together, and that day, I decided to help Jillian tell her story so that the world would better understand her, and children like her.

This book is based on actual events. Those are her thoughts and feelings in her section of the book, although I helped her to express them. Jillian was 11 years old and in the fifth grade when we sat down together and wrote this book, but her story began much earlier.

When Jillian was three years old, she wasn't talking much. She had a noticeable problem playing with other kids and following basic instructions. I enrolled her in an early learning program at a nearby preschool to prepare her for elementary school. When she was five, Jillian was enrolled in elementary school and had a speech and language individualized education plan, which is used to determine any special educational needs of a child that the school is legally obligated to follow. At this age, she was also diagnosed by her pediatrician as having attention-deficit/hyperactivity disorder (ADHD). Her pediatrician recommended medication, and we tried a few, such as Ritalin, Concerta, and Focaline. But I felt as if these medications made her behavior worse. They may have worked for a different child, but they did not work for Jillian. Doctors aren't infallible. There are any number of wrong diagnoses and unhelpful medications prescribed. Always ask questions. You must be very careful, because the decisions we make for our children will affect them throughout their lives.

I was fortunate to have a great relationship with Jillian's pediatrician, who has cared for my children since day one. Parents have a duty to engage in ongoing self-education. Love is essential, but do your due-diligence research as well, because your child's life is in your hands.

I researched ADHD extensively on my own. By the end of Jillian's kindergarten year, I knew that I had to do something, because her condition was affecting her interactions with other students, as well as her academic progress. As Jillian moved into higher grades, I noticed that tasks were becoming more challenging for her both academically and at home. She became more verbally insistent on what she liked and didn't like, and she experienced a succession of sensory issues, which affected, among other areas, her balance and awareness.

She refused to sleep on regular bed sheets, complaining that they hurt her skin. For some odd reason, buttons on clothing would give her anxiety, and she didn't like the texture of jeans. She became extremely picky about her food and refused to eat whatever she deemed "slimy" or "mushy," such as oatmeal and mashed potatoes. The colors of certain foods, such as red and green, disturbed her. Her bread couldn't be broken or sliced before she ate it. As a result of all of this disturbing behavior, she became underweight.

She also started obsessing over rocks, as well as her stuffed animal pets, with whom she sometimes carried on animated conversations. Whenever she received a bruise, she didn't seem to feel a normal amount of pain. She didn't want to become involved with activities outside the home. She spent most of her time in small spaces, such as under her bed or beneath the desk in her room. But she played well with our dog, Major, with whom she also spoke.

The proverbial straw that broke the camel's back was when she removed her seat belt while I was driving her home from school one afternoon. She stuck her head out of the partially open window, and her neck became wedged in the gap. I heard a choking noise coming from the back seat and immediately swerved off the highway, narrowly avoiding an accident. I got her loose and, in a panic, rushed her to the emergency room at the hospital. I'm happy to say that the window didn't break her neck, but after this incident, I never left the rear window open as wide whenever I drove her anywhere.

I knew that Jillian was bright and that it wasn't her hyperactivity that was keeping her back. I remember leaving a jigsaw puzzle on the floor and telling her not to touch it, as we would do it together soon. But she went ahead and put the 2,000-piece puzzle together on her own. I was blown away. So were her siblings—her younger sister, Lindsi, and older brother, Tay.

"How did you do this?" I asked.

"I don't know," she said. "I just did."

Ever since that day, I was convinced that Jillian was intelligent. Over time, I would buy her brain teasers, puzzles, and coloring books, and the way in which she handled every challenge these items presented was amazing. I took her back to the pediatrician and told her how Jillian solved puzzles without undue difficulty. The pediatrician gave me a behavior chart to give to Jillian's teacher to fill out and return to me so that I could give it back to her. After reviewing this chart and conducting her examination, the pediatrician stated unequivocally that Jillian needed to see a neurologist because something was different with her. This diagnosis worried me no end, but I felt that it was a step in the right direction. Ignoring the warning signals would have been a huge mistake.

Subsequently, Jillian had a million-dollar workup; well at least, it felt as if that's how much it cost. She underwent a computed tomography scan of the brain, a neuropsychological test, an IQ test, and an autism diagnosis observation schedule test. After enduring a lengthy waiting period of one year, we finally received feedback, and therapy/counseling was provided. The final diagnosis was Asperger's, which is a form of autism/ASD. However, the neurologist added a hopeful note that "Jillian had a high degree of functionality."

The prolonged experience of waiting on test results was draining and stressful for us both, especially for Jillian, and my hair was slowly turning gray. I wasn't surprised by any aspect of the diagnosis. I knew that Jillian had a medical condition (I prefer not to use the word "problem"), but it was obvious that she still had functionality; I just wasn't sure exactly how this aspect could be measured. All the signs of her condition were crystal clear: underdeveloped social skills, nonverbal behavior, lack of coordination, strict fixation on routines, limited interests, talking to imaginary friends, and so on. It was a long list.

ASD has a wide range of symptoms and levels of disabilities. Like Jillian, some children may have anxiety and ADHD issues. Jillian became very aware of her condition, as I have always been very honest with her. I refused to allow her to think of it as a disability. Instead, I taught her that she was blessed with a special gift that permitted her to be especially sensitive to the reactions of the people she encountered. This may sound like an attempt to make a negative out of a positive, and perhaps it was, but it worked in our case. Jillian seemed to experience a spurt of self-confidence, though she was still uneasy around other people, especially children.

My advice to parents is to tell your children with Asperger's that, yes, they have a tough condition but that it may have benefits, too. This message may be overly subtle and unconvincing, but it's worth a try. As I told Jillian, this world is full of different types of people, just like a rainbow has numerous different colors. Moreover, colors make this world better, just like different types of people do. She nodded, and I felt that she understood.

Of course, as parents, you should be observant of your children in any way that may seem unusual. If your child has displayed any of the behaviors I described, please get them the help they need and truly deserve, and this should be done sooner rather than later. Don't hesitate for fear of receiving depressing results after they undergo a professional examination. However, it is also important to not simply allow a medical professional to give you some pills and send you and your child on your way. Doctors aren't perfect, but you should respect their opinions and suggestions. If specialized help is indicated, you should get it as soon as is feasible. It is also important to note that girls are more likely to be misdiagnosed than boys. Girls tend to want to socialize and be part of a group, even if it is awkward. Boys, conversely, tend to be more isolated.

Coping with Asperger's is obviously difficult for both the child and the parents. Learning what the medical diagnosis is right away is advantageous, though it will seem depressing. It won't be easy, but it will be worth every effort that you can make. Easing the uncertainty and confusion that may show up in your child's mind and behavior is a constant task, but it is one that will pay huge dividends for their future.

CHAPTER II

"Jillian"

My name is Jillian, and I'm 11 years old. I have Asperger's, and at times, I'm a little hyper. People give me anxiety. When I look at the people I'm with, I think that they have anxiety because of me; I can't help it. My mom explained to me what Asperger's is. We even watched a few movies about it. It was hard for me to believe that I did some of the same things that the kids in the movies did. I didn't know that I was different until the kids at school started teasing me sometimes. They called me "weird" and "stupid." Sometimes, it would bother me, but at other times, I ignored what they said and the funny moves they made with their hands when they didn't think I was looking. Fourth and fifth grade were the hardest for me, because that's when I really noticed there were differences between other kids and me, and I didn't understand why this was. My mom always tells me that I have a gift that some kids don't have.

At 11 years old, I finally understood that Asperger's is something that I was born with. It is not contagious; it is not a disease that you can catch from me. I think, act, and learn differently from other people. All people with Asperger's aren't the same either. We all have different qualities. Boy and girl "Aspies"—a term that is short for Asperger's and is used to describe people with the condition—differ from one another. My mom said that Asperger's is a form of autism, which is a kind of disorder. Some people are low-functioning, and some are high-functioning like me. Mom insists that being high-functioning is a great sign. I sure hope so. This disorder has a lot of different parts. Aspies can be better or worse when it comes to being with other kids or adults, meaning that some are better with social skills and some worse. Some repeat themselves more than others, and some are better at showing their thoughts and feelings without speaking. I don't know where I fit in. I feel as if I need to be better when it comes to all these characteristics, but I'm not sure how I can do this. My mom always tells me it will come with experience,

I would like to share my world with you so that you can see and understand who I am. My best friend's name is Timmy. I do everything with him. But my mom won't allow me to take him to school. Mom describes Timmy as a stuffed animal dog, but to me, he is as real as I am. I have a lot of friends that only I can see. But my mom makes them stay at home whenever we leave the house for school. Sometimes, I go with her when she goes shopping. I enjoy seeing all the things in the stores.

I eat only certain foods, as I'm very picky, and I know it now. I don't eat slimy or mushy foods. Sometimes, I can eat the same thing for weeks or months at a time. I like everything done the same way. If my mom doesn't serve my food the same way, I won't eat it; so, I must remind her. She's very patient with me most of the time. But I know that I get on her nerves sometimes. I feel bad about this, but I can't help myself.

Certain sounds bother me very much. But the sounds I like or want to hear don't bother me.

When I come home from school, I do the same thing every day. I have a routine, and I don't like change. I don't like it when my mom adds something to our daily routine.

Certain smells hurt my nose and make me want to puke. I smell things that others don't smell. Is my nose different, too?

When I'm nervous, I start to pick my skin, and my hands begin to fidget. Sometimes, I'm told to act my age, but when normal things make you nervous, see how you react! Will I be different next year when I'm 12? Will I ever be normal like everyone else?

Sometimes, when I'm forced to do something I don't want to do, or if I can't explain my feelings, I have a meltdown. I just can't control how I behave, and everything happens so quickly. Before I know it, I've done something that worries my mother. Mom then holds me tightly in her arms, rocks me as if I were still a baby, and tells me that everything will be okay. This helps me a lot.

The biggest struggle I have is communicating with other children. I don't understand kids; they confuse me.

I try hard to fit in, especially with the boys, because we like to play the same games.

My mom says that when I try too hard to fit in, things go wrong. So, I prefer to play by myself; I don't like group activities. It's hard to tell whether someone is smiling because they like me or because they are laughing at me. I also don't know when people are joking with me or when they're being sarcastic. Having animals as friends is much easier.

Mom says that I need to pay more attention to people personal space She thinks that maybe I get too physically close to people. But how close is close? She can't answer this question. I can't remember everything she tells me to do and feel, though I try to be good.

Mom makes me practice looking at her because I don't like looking people in the eyes. Maybe I do it the wrong way or for too long. I don't know, but I get some funny looks from other kids. One day during after care at school, I was trying to practice staring at people. But the kids kept asking me what I was looking at and they started to move away from me.

I wanted so badly for these kids to like me, so I started dancing and mimicking characters from my video game. The kids were laughing, so I thought they liked me. Then, they started trying to record me with their cell phones. Finally, the prime time after-care teacher stopped them. I thought the kids liked me, but they were just laughing at me. I don't really understand how to be when I want someone to like me. People are very confusing.

My teachers were always very nice. I could see that they wanted to be patient with me, but they acted as if I was mentally slow, and I'm not—not too slow, anyway. I can learn. I read, write, and do okay in most subjects. I love computer class, and I like to draw. The teacher even complimented me on some of my drawings of animals. But I don't like school too much. I like some things, such as computers, but overall, I prefer to be home with Timmy and my dog, Major. My teacher talks so fast, and he says so many things that I can't keep up. Then, I get nervous and confused. I have trouble understanding everything that is said, and I'm too embarrassed to raise my hand, so I pretend to understand. Certain expressions that everyone else seems to understand just confuse me. I'm not sure what's real and what isn't. People say that I take things literally, but if I don't know what someone means, I'm left confused.

Mom always says that I should be myself no matter what and that I should be comfortable in my own skin. Sometimes, I wonder, *who else's skin could I be comfortable in?*

But I have never asked her this. She said that some people will like me, some won't, and that this is okay. It's like this for everyone. Mom says that I'm perfect the way I am and that if someone wants to be my friend, they will accept me for who I am.

Life would be much better if I could stay home and cuddle with my best friend, Timmy, and my dog, Major. I love animals. I like them more than people. At school, my resource teacher sometimes lets me stay inside during recess. I love it because I get to spend more time playing games on the device Mom bought me—a cell phone. She taught me how to use it when I was in second grade, including how to call her when I need her.

I love going to the park. I like to climb. Looking down from trees makes me feel strong; instead of looking up at people, I can look down on them. I find the biggest tree to climb, and I stay there. One day when we were at the park, I was sitting in a big tree watching everyone, and Mom began to panic because she couldn't find me. When I yelled out where I was, she was shocked to see me so high up in the tree. It was awesome, but Mom didn't think so. I climbed down, and she hugged me as if I had fallen from the sky.

I have a sister named Lindsi, but we call her "Honie." Mom said that I gave her the name Honie when she was born, so everyone calls her by this name. Honie is two years younger than I am, but she acts like she's my big sister. She and I are very different. She has a lot of friends, and I don't. I like playing games, and she likes texting her friends. We each have our own computer. Learning how to use the computer is fun. Our older brother, Tay, is very good with computers I love beating him in computer games.

Sometimes, Honie helps me with my jigsaw puzzles, but she's not that great with puzzles. What I love most about Honie is that she understands me and accepts me for who I am.

Honie dresses differently from me. Every time she gets dressed, she thinks she's in a fashion show. I'm very picky when it comes to clothing. Some clothes are uncomfortable for me and irritate my skin. I don't like buttons or scratchy clothes. I like to feel soft, plush material against my skin. I don't like sleeping on my bedsheets because they irritate my skin. I sleep on a plush blanket. Unlike my sister, I am not a fancy dresser.

I'm not good at coordinating clothes, and I don't care if what I wear doesn't match. I just like being comfortable. Most of the time, Mom picks out my clothes, but this doesn't stop Honie from making suggestions.

When my mom isn't at work or busy, we do puzzles together. I like puzzles and brainteasers, and I'm good at them. I can sit all day working on my puzzles until I'm finished. Things that other people consider boring fascinate me. Mom says I like to go on and on about things. But if I like something, what's wrong with saying so? Rocks and dinosaurs are my favorite things. I like telling people about my rocks, but sometimes Mom says people don't want to hear about rocks all the time.

Mom also says that I'm too honest. I don't think about what I say before I say it. If what I'm saying is true, I don't understand why I can't say it. I do tell lies sometimes, but Mom says I'm not good at it, so I need to ensure that I tell her the truth even when doing so might hurt me. How does someone become good at telling lies? And why would anyone want to be good at that? But I don't ask these kinds of questions. I used to get funny looks when I did, so I don't anymore.

I love it when Tay comes to visit. He's in his 20s and lives nearby with his friends. Tay and I have the same father, but we have different mothers. My brother is supercool. He plays with me, and he lets me eat all the junk food I want. I love when he comes to visit.

I wish Tay could live with us, because he loves playing video games with me all night. I hate when he's working because I hardly ever get to see him, but we text a lot. My brother loves me so much that he tattooed my name on his chest. How cool is that?

I may not have a lot of friends, but I have my sister, my brother, my mom, and my best friend, Timmy. I can be myself around them. I am who I am, and that's all I know how to be. Please don't try to change me. It's hard enough trying to fit into a world I will never understand. Sometimes, I feel like a visitor from another planet, because I don't see the world like everyone else does. But it's true that everyone wants to be accepted whether they have Asperger's or not. I understand Mom better now. We are all special and unique in our own way. I have emotions like everyone else, but I'm not always sure which ones to show in certain situations. If you see me at school or outside of school and you wonder why I act the way I do, please don't call me stupid or weird. I'm just being the only person I know how to be.

I've shared my story. Now, try to imagine yourself in my shoes. Imagine trying to fit into a world in which people will never understand you and see how hard it can be. Mom says that God created us all different. He decided to make me with Asperger's, and I'm okay with that now, as Mom also says that life is like a puzzle: We need to figure out its rough edges, and then the rest will fall into place.

CHAPTER III

"Conclusion"

Jillian is now 13 years old and is attending middle school. She's growing up fast both physically and mentally. She still has all the attributes of Asperger's. Nevertheless, she's doing well at school and has decided that she wants to go to college. This was truly wonderful news. She's especially interested in becoming a veterinarian, as she loves animals. Her teachers are also supportive, and one teacher said that she would gladly write a letter of recommendation when it's time for Jillian to apply to universities. That time is still far off, so I hope that when the time comes, this teacher will still be teaching and will remember the promise she made to Jillian.

Jillian hasn't discovered boys yet, but I'm sure her days of dating aren't far off. I don't think I'm too strict. She doesn't have any real girlfriends, and she isn't part of a group or clique. But she says she's much more comfortable interacting with kids her age. This is also welcome news.

In all things, Jillian is showing signs of coping successfully with Asperger's and becoming as normal a preteenager as can be expected. I am now more confident about her future. Honie is also doing well, and Tay has secured a full-time job at a furniture store. I'm still busy working in the medical field and taking care of my girls. I'm blessed with a wonderful family, and I thank God all the time.

I hope this book has been useful for readers who are facing similar situations due to Asperger's. The road may be difficult, but the passage will be infinitely better if you exercise love, understanding, and an abundance of patience.

Jillian is looking forward to sharing her middle-school experience with you, so look out for *Happy to Be an Aspie 2*.

Recommended Books & Web Sites

The Complete Guide to Asperger's Syndrome – Tony Attwood

Look Me in the Eyes: My Life with Asperger's – John Elder Robinson

Asperger's Syndrome: A Guide for Parents and Professionals – Tony Attwood

1001 Great Ideas for Teaching and Raising Children with Autism or Asperger's – Ellen Notbohm and Veronica Zysk

Autismwomensnetwork.org

Aspennj.org

thecolorofautism.org

APPENDIX

Individualized Educational Program (IEP)

• The Individuals with Disabilities Act, which is a federal law, requires public schools to create individualized education plans for children receiving special educational services. The program is designed to address each child's unique learning issues and should include specific educational goals for him or her, as well as how the goals of the program will be measured.

Autism Diagnostic Observation Schedule (ADOS)

• ADOS is an instrument that is used to diagnose and assess autism. The protocol consists of structured and semi-structured tasks involving social interaction between the examiner and the subject. This procedure takes anywhere from 30 to 60 minutes. Subsequently, the findings are categorized for the identification and assessment of autistic symptoms.

Attention-Deficit/Hyperactivity Disorder (ADHD)

• In most cases, the exact cause of this neurodevelopment disorder is unknown. It affects boys much more than girls. It is characterized by problems with paying attention, excessive activity unrelated to what is going on, and general difficulty behaving in an age-appropriate manner.